THIS COLORING BOOK BELONGS TO

This coloring book is dedicated to my friend Laura Smith. She is azookeeper at the Knoxville Zoo dedicated to caring for their red pandas.

Southern Creative Books
Church Hill TN, 37642
2022 Designed by Kimberly McEachen
Like us on Facebook at Southern Creative Books
Visit our Amazon Author's Page at Southern Creative Books